the flap pamphlet series

Small Change

flap

open, read, turn

Small Change

the flap pamphlet series (No. 8)
Printed and Bound in the United Kingdom

Published by the flap series, 2013
the pamphlet series of flipped eye publishing
All Rights Reserved

Cover Design by Petraski
Series Design © flipped eye publishing, 2010
Author Photo © Yemisi Blake

First Edition
Copyright © Miriam Nash 2013

ISBN-13: 978-1-905233-41-0
Editorial work for this series is supported by the Arts Council of England

LOTTERY FUNDED

Small Change

Miriam Nash

Contents | *Small Change*

I

Iona Sky

You can eat the sky above Iona
like a mango: red, succulent,
cut through with green; colours
of another earth caught up
in northern light: sugarcane,
ripe lemon, deep hibiscus blush.

Hush. The years grow heavy,
burn, blossom, explode
as paintballs in the blue. Up spring
the spiked black railings,
Staffa's old brick teeth, the distance.
Me in the wheelbarrow, daddy pushing,
noses of peat and bonfire. I pluck
a fresh round gulp, swollen and damp:
Mull air, olive on the tongue.

Morning Milking

6am, the day a pale sharp blue,
   down the track, my hand in my dad's.
Everything waking in frosted outlines,
   me in my wellies and bobble-hat
     walking the morning.
Into the byre:
sleepy and deep with dung,
   mixed with the mist of breath
     in the moo of the morning.
I stand on the gate, watch
   as my dad takes the teats
     between fingers and eases drips
from the udders, sending the shudders
   up and down my spine
     in time with the milking.
And the droplets of milk
   and of mud and of love
cling in the air of the clean blue morning
   stinging the two red dots of my cheeks
     bright as my boots and bobbling hat.
Silent, I watch
   wanting to seal and stamp this moment
     in an envelope addressed to my older self
there, on the mat of a London flat
   next to the semi-skimmed pasteurised, saying:
you were once this child of the morning
   you can become her again.

Essentials

No rose tinted tea-lights for us,
we hoarded solid slabs of light.
Each one ten hours worth of evening:

a meal, a bedtime story,
the nuanced eyes of arguments,
the washing up.

We knew the flickering of lamps,
the gnarled wind's talons at the wires,
its whoosh of sudden darkness.

Wax bricks arrived in bulk
with rice and sugar, immutable as marble
till we coaxed them back to liquid,

poured their shifting bodies into moulds.
At night, our homemade candles
stood like sentinels, positioned

for the sweep of match to box.
One family, we'd crowd their flames
while slates swooped from the roof

like leaden bats. The house swayed
on its hinges, a frightened mother,
belly pulled inwards.

When a bulb blows, when strip lights stutter
when tube lamps stumble out in tunnels,
when the BBC broadcasts from Gaza

I think of them, our fat light towers,
how we needed them as much as laughter.
While outside, the landscape mutated,

another monster cracked and hungered,
its own electric flare illuminating us:
tiny, clinging to wax and wick
in the mouth of its wake.

In the Beginning

...a Balkan brass band,
time begins
   on a seven/eight beat.
A moan,
   rising from the horn's throat,
      the hum of tuba,
   clash of trumpets
on the flick/boom of the drum.

Somewhere a navel is twisting,
   infinitesimally tiny,
infinitely hot,
   a knot
in the pulsing dark.
   Winding the emptiness,
   a procession,
      free arms beckoning a rhythm,
   a wedding dance,
breath shaped to metal song.

The angels are caterwauling,
   coils of spinning sound,
catherine wheels
     so piercing
       they could break
a grown man's chest.

Over the unformed sky
       instruments scatter,
cling in constellations,
          shimmer.

In a basement bar across town,
   over voices and the chink
   of glass on glass,
     the band pick up their brass.
It swells
   from the depths of a sax,
     from the neck of a shining horn.
In the base of my chest
a universe is born.

Head Space

My grandmother hid her brain
in a cupboard, behind stacked plates.
She brought it kitchen scraps,
fed it stories, gossip, TV facts,
her daughters' phonecalls, forecasts,
foreign words, whole chapters
out of novels, recipes for love wounds
or smoked mackerel, once
an erotic letter, pulsing under breath.
Her brain inhaled these gifts
as moisture swells to raincloud.
Eye pressed to hinge, I watched
as, camouflaged within white china,
it grew to the size of a sky.

Wonderful

This word, your word, ripples my skin
like the pleasure of a tickle.
For wild blue Swedish skies,

for the bear hug of your garden chair,
for a whiff of wet firs breathed deep
or a well baked fish, you opened,

wound *wonderful* from throat to sunlight,
your prayer to a well lived day.
Spring came when you christened

the first bud of a crocus. I mouthed
three syllables to match your lips.
        One autumn, when the sun sank

red and gold behind dark trees and dust,
you spluttered.
The word inched forward,

pushed past larynx, vocal tract,
lurching like a frosted engine,
wheezing to weak utterance.

Indoors, it would still sound:
a bunch of daffodils, a grandchild's poem,
the touch of a nurse's palm.

In the end I learned to see it rising in the silence
before a cough,
a faint glow around closed lips.

Her Place

No headstone marks her place,
only a mess of wild Swedish strawberries,

accidental, reaching their tentacles
far across the soil to touch another

sleeping mound. A ladybird
crawls round a leaf; a tiny sign of her,

come to wink hello with insect eyes.
I bend to let it creep into my hand,

feel its dot of crimson body quiver
in my palm. She lifts her wings

and floats away, as if this field
were any other field.

Small Change

They say royal heads sank
in the coat linings of tramps,

that their weight was promise.
You could never know where they'd been,

children held them in their mouths
like secrets. I saw one once

at a museum, one of the last.
The queen on its face was fat

and double chinned, as if she might roll off.
I'd expected rust, a murky glimpse

at how time eats, but this thing shone
like it was made tomorrow;

I couldn't imagine it wet,
between the ridges of a palm. They say

they disappeared from bus stops,
then from pockets, their tiny bodies

called 'unruly', jingle silenced.
Slot machines sat empty; no one came

to wish at the fountains, or if they did
they brought their credit cards.

Only the tooth fairy kept a few
faded coppers, salvaged for the sons

and daughters of historians.
They couldn't be exchanged

for anything. Little aliens,
they stared from under pillows.

Even they could tell they stank
of another time.

We Can Still Dance
for Evie Nash

While Mum was getting change,
we danced a Russian dance in the car park,
next to the fat black tank from World War II.

You stamped your camel-coloured uggs
in perfect time, directing the steps
as you used to, two years old in the living room

where we beat saucepans at the centre of a world
we built from clothes racks and old fruit boxes,
your wide voice joining mine in a yelled song.

After all the years, the slammed doors,
the times we let nothing in
and hugged our cold knees in the dark, alone,

to know we can still dance like this
is enough for me to hold to;
linking my arms in yours, following your feet.

Burn Mark

I always envied boys
who'd run their fingers

through a naked flame
as coolly as I'd stroke a cat.

I never knew the trick
of pinching out a wick

or saw them lick the tips
of forefingers behind my back.

I felt the sting of black
red heat upon my skin,

the burning crumb of ash,
its smoky ring imprinted

on my thumb; still see
the cackles on their lips.

II

Half Size

for Lawry Gold

Those afternoons we may or may not have spent strumming, you placing giant fingers over frets, me picking out a tune. There is the instrument between us, belly in my lap, neck in the flex of your hand, the smell of fresh paint over damp, the off-white light. Maybe a window is open, shouts from the pub next door, those blasts of seaweed air. Easy to imagine a pose and call it ours, to taste a Simon & Garfunkel song, though I don't know if we ever played 'The Boxer'. The guitar vanished from its hook – perhaps I didn't play enough, or maybe it had always been a loan. What a liar I am, searching for a perfect moment. All I find are your hairy hands, a guitar in my arms like a child, a bare patch of wallpaper.

Reverb

or Can't Recall

how it felt to hate your mother
to twist and wrench your navel
hand her the stub
skunk anansie yelling everything
you want to yell in reverb
your veins taut strings
how hunger is a weapon
your barbed wire or alsatian
inside you so much air
you hardly need to breathe
you sit in vaulted rooms
an apple bite the first sign of asbestos
your tongue curling the corners
of a mouth you never really liked
thinking even bad love
must be better than nothing

Fifteen

from a photograph of Alexandros Grigoropoulos,
shot dead by police in Athens, 6 December 2008.

He looks like the boys I knew at 15,
scraggly hair flopped to hide
brow-punctures, picked spots, bleeding;
boys who mastered bar chords late at night,
sliding frets with fingers thicker
than I could ever hope for;
boys who flaunted t-shirts
from their fathers' old rebellions
(the ones before slick briefcases, or absence).

Back then, we shook with the ecstasy of *No*.
G.M. crops were slashed, pollen fog fell
from field to schoolyard. We yearned
for fever, stretched our hands to catch.
Outside the Labour Party Conference,
we threw on cow costumes, plunged
into a beating, breathing crowd,
flung nursery rhyme slogans, loud
on the five o'clock news. Imagine one of us
had broken herd, and hurled a stone.

Love Poem to Hunger

after Catherine Pierce

I know you have other lovers.
Girls who calculate the rate
of grist to penny while you
thrash, a giant eel inside them.
Children whose bellies
are sacks of you. When you
roll in at 2am, you stink
of the fox in the garden.
Your breath is paving stones
licked after acid rain.
Come, I've lined the sheets
with crumbs. I want
your wet croak in my ear,
your lurch in my ribs –
each intake sounds so
like a promise.

Stepmother

(i)

In French you are 'beautiful-mother',
no children at your wedding, no thermos
in your kitchen, not one moth
between your coats. You're words like pert
and delicate, curbing all protest
in the hook of a smile, your teeth
look best on beaches, storm
clouds aren't your style. Stop
me. All my tales of you are terse.
Your mirror's a liar, your hope
is the shape of a home.

(ii)

You're here
and entirely other.

Your body less fragrant, pores
sticky as mine. I mope,

listen for thunder. You sort
through our boxes, pluck a dead stem

from a pot. I call you a temp
in this house, test

your resistance, then tether
myself to your leg. I could smother

you under your pillow. I could let you be more.

Arsenal

All night I cradled guns, slick metal hulks
I wouldn't have the vocab for awake,
but there, I knew enough gun words to floor
the index of a firearm handbook,
as if I'd stored an arsenal for years.
I loaded, plugged them in your cavities:
foreign ones I'd stolen from museums,
archaic pearls I savoured under tongue,
a hoard of dirty beauties extracted
from my grandfather's dead mouth, finally
your words, your favourite curses, TV quotes,
your nicknames for me, cute and nasty.

Your nostrils, the whites of your eyes are dumb.
I've emptied my mouth; I reach for my gun.

Faithful

One day he'll crave new stories,
shave his hair, join the gym,
wake with a new species
of happiness, in other arms.
Anything to hew his body
from the family plot.
The most reliable source of love
will sag - I learnt this early.

But I can hear my father,
who is still my father,
treading the wooden steps to Mum's
with plans: weekends,
a spare room, London Zoo, his old
impatience, birthday cards heavy
with pride. Years later, hunger
and lover are gone. I trace oak rings
at his table, crafted by my own
great-grandfather's hands, now his.
He holds my shoulders, rocks.

Imprint

If nothing of us lasts past seven years,
each speck of skin replaced, old cells reborn,
then soon, the crisscross lines inside your palm
where I pretended to read kids, careers,
won't recognise my thumbprints anymore.
This fleck of face, that furthest tip of tongue,
whole parts of us will never know they touched,
nights when our tiny room swelled up with breath,
till one window exhaled for us at dawn.
Then, will our new skin falter, taste sudden
cold, unknown? Will bones be what we dig for?
When our two chests press, stranger to stranger,
our particles in motion, trembling, raw,
will my flesh blaze to yours, for seven more?

Aubade

Singapore

We sleep too near the equator
for me to convince you
the yellowing of curtains is streetlight.
This sky is clockwork, dawn punches
into its shift, swallows the city
in one. Half-waking, I could try
to trick you, say we're in Rome
or Southampton, where morning
comes gently, shifting its hour
through the year like a child
growing tall on the sly. But we lie
at the edges, sheets heavy
between us, already awake.

Notes &
Acknowledgements

Notes

- In **Reverb**, the subtitle 'Can't Recall' is taken from the Skunk Anansie song *Comfort of Strangers*.
- **Fifteen** was written in response to a photograph which appeared online on the *Boston Globe*'s Big Picture website on December 15 2008.
- **Stepmother** makes use of Terrance Hayes' 'gram of &s' form, in which each line of an eleven line poem ends with a word made up of letters from the title word. These 'anagram' end words must have at least four letters. See Terrance Hayes' *Hip Logic*.

Acknowledgements

Thanks to the following publications in which some of these poems (or versions of these poems) first appeared: *Brand Literary Magazine, Daydream Magazine, Domestic Cherry, Generations Literary Journal, Magma Poetry, Popshot Magazine, The Battered Suitcase* and the anthologies **The Freedom of Paper and Ink** (Salt), **The Loose Muse Anthology** and **The Shuffle Anthology**. My heartfelt thanks to the Vineyard poets, Jacob Sam-La Rose and Nii Ayikwei Parkes and to my family, especially Christina, Mark, Evie, Treya, Patrick, Amanda and Hristo.

Lightning Source UK Ltd.
Milton Keynes UK
UKOW02f0843120816

280542UK00004B/13/P